WAKING UP
with "PURPOSE"

WAKING UP
with
"PURPOSE"

*Looking unto Jesus the author and finisher of our faith.
Hebrews 12:2*

JAMYE L. HILL

Xulon Press

Xulon Press
2301 Lucien Way #415
Maitland, FL 32751
407.339.4217
www.xulonpress.com

© 2021 by Jamye L. Hill

All rights reserved solely by the author. The author guarantees all contents are original and do not infringe upon the legal rights of any other person or work. No part of this book may be reproduced in any form without the permission of the author.

Due to the changing nature of the Internet, if there are any web addresses, links, or URLs included in this manuscript, these may have been altered and may no longer be accessible. The views and opinions shared in this book belong solely to the author and do not necessarily reflect those of the publisher. The publisher therefore disclaims responsibility for the views or opinions expressed within the work.

Unless otherwise indicated, Scripture quotations taken from the King James Version (KJV) – *public domain*.

Paperback ISBN-13: 978-1-66283-036-5
Ebook ISBN-13: 978-1-66283-037-2

*I dedicate this book
in their memory,
Jacquelyn A. Hill
& Ruben D. Thomas...*

SPECIAL THANKS:

To my wonderful seven children,

I know my journey has not always been easy in discovering my purpose.

You have watched me endure some of the most challenging and difficult times in our lives.

You all have been my inspiration for living to always achieve higher goals for myself.

You have been my support and my strength through it all.

Waking up with "Purpose"

Thank you for not allowing me to give up when times got hard or when I could not see my way out of some of the cloudiest times of my life.

There were times when the lights got turned off and we had to make the best of what we had and endure it all, even staying in some of the most unlivable hotels when we lost our home.

We have been through a lot, and I am thankful for each and every one of you. You are my heartbeats.

To the next generation...my twenty-plus grandkids,

I write this book in honor of you all, and I pray that my journey will lead you to a life of fellowship and success with God in discovering who you are in Him...

Special thanks:

because you are the next generation and nation all by yourselves. My prayer is that you all will become the light of this world.

To my beautiful daughters-in-law, Thank you for your love and support through it all. And to my siblings, thank you for your love and support and your words of encouragement that have kept me along the way.

To my Agape church family,

My pastor Darly and First Lady Legena Collins. God has blessed me with His very best. He said that He would give us shepherds after His own heart.

Your love and prayers have pulled me through some of the most difficult and darkest times in my life.

Waking up with "Purpose"

Thank you both with much love and respect.

To Missionary Karen Anderson, who said to me, "Never let no one put you in a box,"

Your words of wisdom have kept me moving forward on my journey.

To Mother Sandra McDonald,

Thank you for speaking the Word of God into my spirit, saying, "Never despise small beginnings."

To the endless amount of family and friends who have encouraged and kept me lifted up in your prayers... thank you all.

TABLE OF CONTENTS

CHAPTER ONE:
Purpose *1*

CHAPTER TWO:
Respond to Purpose. *7*

CHAPTER THREE:
The Call for Purpose *13*

CHAPTER FOUR:
What Happened to Us?. *17*

CHAPTER FIVE:
Have We Forgotten Our Way? . . . *23*

CHAPTER SIX:
Understanding Purpose. *29*

CHAPTER SEVEN:
Let's Look at the Church *35*

CHAPTER EIGHT:
Faith Comes by Hearing
the Word of God *43*

Introduction

PURPOSE

Your life's purpose consists of the central motivation of your life.

The reason you get up in the morning, your purpose guides your life decisions, influences your behavior, shapes your goals, and offers a sense of direction and meaning.

Living your life's purpose gives you happiness and more control over your life, hence reducing the stress on your body's systems.

Therefore, alleviating these stresses through knowing and living your life's purpose will inevitably lead to better mental and physical health.

The purpose of life is focused on spiritual growth and service to humanity.

Human beings are viewed as intrinsically spiritual beings.

People's lives in this material world provide extended opportunities to grow and develop divine qualities and virtues.

...God has plans for our lives!

God is God, and He works all things, including your life, according to His purpose.

Nothing can happen without God ordaining it. Psalm 57:2 says, "I cried out to the most high God, who fulfills his purpose for me."

This is key in understanding God's purpose for your life.

It seems that we have forgotten our way because of the heaviness of life's issues.

The spirit of depression has taken its position, so now we are just settling and not expecting more—that abundance of life that Jesus has already paid for with His life. Jesus said that He is the way, the truth, and the life and the only way to the Father. So, when we come to service and do not acknowledge Jesus, what we are doing is in vain.

Waking up with "Purpose"

The people of God have settled in their mindset that salvation is the only thing there is, even though we attend church service for many years!

There is no real connection to the Lord.

We enter in heavy or out of tradition and from the outer courts.

I hear people saying things like, "Service was good," and, "The spirit was high."

But are we coming in expecting God to show up in all His glory?

So, like the children of Israel, we wander around in our own wilderness.

As I began to write, I started thinking of my own family members and myself... like my mother and brother, who died so prematurely, not fully understanding who God was in their lives and that He had a divine purpose for them and Jesus had already made the way.

Like so many, they had no relationship with Him—they knew of Him but not the power within.

I had to watch two of the most important people in the world to me suffer while they were dying, but during their time of departure, the Holy Spirit reminded me of the sinner's prayer to lead them both in prayer for forgiveness on their way home (heaven).

That's how much God loved them both, even though they never experienced Him in His glory.

Waking up with "Purpose"

That experience left me feeling hopeless because I was saved and knew of God.

I went to church and served in many departments.

But as time went on and years passed by, I discovered that I myself had no real fellowship with my Heavenly Father. This experience made me want to know more of Him because I was expecting God to heal my brother and mother.

Years continued to pass by. One day, I was attending a service and heard these words: "God only responds to His Word."

So, the thirst in me begin.

Can it be because we are not abiding or are not in constant fellowship with God, the One who created you and me?

Chapter One

PURPOSE

I was compelled to fellowship with the Holy Spirit in the darkest and most painful time of my life, a time that was so depressing that all I wanted to do was have a pity party and die.

I could barely keep my head above water and wondered why this was happening to me.

Waking up with "Purpose"

In the most trying times of my life, I could not believe or imagine that the Father would call me to write this book in the state of mind that I was in to bring a sense of purpose with understanding to the believers of Jesus Christ, including me.

In that moment of my life, I thought all hope was gone while the tears were rolling down my face; but yet, in the midst of my tears and pain and sorrow, I found my purpose for living. Hallelujah!

Yes, I had something to look forward to now. Sometimes I would fight within myself because of where I was—no job, a computer that wasn't functioning properly—but I knew that God had called me to become His vessel.

The call for purpose is a faithful walk in the supernatural. We cannot see it or feel it with our natural senses, and our emotions can cause us to walk away prematurely because we do not understand the ways of God.

When God has placed a desire in us, He will lead on the right path.

So many times, that path seems unfruitful or hopeless. I have witnessed many of God's children aborting their purpose because they could not believe that they were called to do something unexpected or that had never been done before. Even in my own experience, I have walked away because I too had no knowledge of God's purpose for my life, which caused me to wander around in my wilderness for years.

Waking up with "Purpose"

The waiting can become unbearable. Therefore, we go back to our own ways of doing things.

This way of thinking will lead us to a life of despair, pain, sorrow, loneliness, and feelings of abandonment:

A life that is lost or has an absence of hope.

So, we start doing things unknowingly or unintentionally.

Not being aware of what is happening, we can then begin to indulge in things like drugs, drinking, or even prostitution as low self-esteem creeps in and overtakes us. This causes our minds to become idle.

The Bible speaks against being idle-minded, telling us what to think about instead (Phil. 4:8).

You see, this walk is an extraordinary walk with God. It will allow you to understand Him more than ever because it is a new walk. We go from faith to faith in Him, meaning that we are supposed to grow and not stay the same.

Each new level in Him will cause us to step out of our comfort zone and trust Him more because there is a new level that awaits us.

It is so important that we seek Him on a daily basis for instructions on what to do, where to go, and how to give accordingly.

Chapter Two

RESPOND TO PURPOSE

Many are not responding to their call for purpose in their lives because they do not know that they have a purpose in the kingdom of Jesus Christ. We are of a royal priesthood (1 Peter 2:9).

Knowing our purpose in this life will open up doors in different areas of our lives that we never could imagine. Our health and the way we live will be at

a higher mark than those who have no sense of purpose.

Purpose brings more clarity, and therefore, our aim will be higher.

We then become aware of the inner small voice or that pull for something higher that drives us to answering the call for purpose.

The Lord has always used purpose to lead His children to achieve the supernatural.

The supernatural is a Holy Spirit-empowered life. It is a life that depends on God for wisdom and strength. The Spirit alone gives life, and He alone can enable believers to keep God's commands.

Now, let's briefly take a look at the Bible.

The Bible tells the story of the children of Israel, God's chosen people, and how they overcame many trials while discovering their purpose.

The Bible is our blueprint for living. It shares stories of those who lived a life of faith and trusted God, even when they could not understand the "hows" or "whys" of what was going on. They understood that God is all-knowing and all-powerful, and they had the faith to believe and endure the process.

Without being rooted in the true Word of God, we will not be able to stand the test of faith.

I am not talking about the kind of faith we see today…centered on touch and feeling.

Waking up with "Purpose"

I reference the faith that Hebrews 11:1 talks about: "Now faith is the substance of things hope for, the evidence of things not seen."

For years, I have witnessed the body of Christ not living according to the full gospel. So, I began to seek God for understanding as to why the church was not in this position when authority and power over the enemy have already been given (Matt. 28: 18-20).

We have become a group of people who operate off the belief that if we do not see or feel something, then it must not be true.

When God delivered the children of Israel out of bondage, He led them through the wilderness.

Now we are talking about the Almighty God who could have led them straight to the promised land, but He didn't!

He knew what they needed in order for them to develop a faith walk with Him.

He was a cloud by day and a pillar of fire by night that guided them after their departure from Egypt (Ex. 13:21-22).

This was the first miracle that God used to show His children that He was all-powerful.

He demonstrated this to show His faithfulness and teach us that He will never leave nor forsake His people.

You see, the wilderness had purpose for the Israelites...yes, a place that appeared to have nothing.

Waking up with "Purpose"

It was a place of unseen fruit.

Right now, you might be asking, "What are you trying to say?"

What I am saying is that if you find yourselves like the children of Israel, having nothing or having to start all over again with the same trial repeating year after year, maybe God is trying to develop a faith walk in you. Do not become dismayed. Purpose is at work.

Chapter Three

THE CALL FOR PURPOSE

Many times, we see the fame of a person and not the suffering he or she has had to endure—people like Bishop T.D. Jakes, Joyce Meyers, Joel Osteen, Dr. Juanita Bynum, and so many more.

God has used them to influence the church and the world today in the knowledge of His Word on how they overcame their trials.

But they had to endure the valley or wilderness experience before God could use them.

They had to endure longsuffering and trust that God's Word was true in order for them to come out and climb higher to the mountaintop.

They discovered their purpose while going through the wilderness or valley (notice that I said "while" going through). They kept on moving in God, believing that there had to be more.

We see their fame now but not the struggles they had to endure to get to where they are in God.

The Father meets every individual where he or she is in life, meaning that we do not wait to come to Him until we get clean or right in a sense. Come to Him with your addictions or habits and bring it all to the altar.

He will meet us right where we are in life in order to get us to go where He is calling us in our purpose to be used for the kingdom.

There is always suffering before ministry: "But you, keep your head in all situations, endure hardship, do the work of an evangelist, discharge all the duties of your ministry" (2 Tim. 4:5).

All Christians suffer. Either you have, or you will. We must go through many tribulations to enter the kingdom of God (Acts 14:22).

But like so many, when trials come, we are not able to stand the test of faith because we are not rooted in His Word. We have no fellowship with Him.

But the Bible says about those who have a relationship with Him: "That person is like a tree planted by the rivers of waters, which yields its fruits in due season and whose leaf does not wither, whatever they do prospers" (Ps. 1:3). Amen!

Now after reading that verse, I began to look at the church of Jesus Christ and noticed that we are not fully operating or functioning as the church with all power and authority.

Chapter Four

WHAT HAPPENED TO US?

I have watched the issues of life consume believers in such a way that they begin to do things their own way.

Therefore, they are not truly operating in the faith.

I have witnessed people getting second or third jobs to make ends meet, so on Sunday mornings, they are at work instead of fellowshipping together with other believers to receive a word from the Lord.

He told us in His Word, "Fail not to assemble together" (Heb. 10:25).

As I began to fellowship with the people as to where they were as believers, this is the response that I got:

"Oh, I don't do the church thing anymore."

Lord, help us. We have turned away from God!

Our purpose has been lost within ourselves, and we have forgotten the way.

Jesus said that He is the way, the truth, and the life.

He is the only way to the Father.

The Father said that no one can come to Him unless we come in the name of His Son Jesus Christ, the Savior of the world.

When we go to Him, we must first believe and receive Jesus as Lord over our lives, taking our position back as His body with the authority, dominion, and power that has already been given to us, His church!

As I reflect on the movie called **The Passion of the Christ,** *I believe it was a movie made to really show us the suffering that our Lord and Savior endured for us.*

It was a movie that showed the effects of the torture and beatings He received.

Through it all, He never said a word, even though He experienced longsuffering that no man has ever faced.

Jesus knew His purpose for coming and dying.

He was the ultimate sacrifice for the world, even though it became unbearable for Him.

Scripture tells us that Jesus prayed in the garden of Gethsemane (Matt. 26:36-39), "If it is possible, let this cup pass me by," because it became overwhelming.

The Lord knew He needed to suffer (His purpose) for the sins of all humanity.

Now, He did not want to suffer, but He chose to obey the Father and fulfill

His purpose for you and me by going to Calvary.

Jesus came not only for salvation—He came to give us so much more.

He said, "I come to give you life and life abundantly" (John 10:10).

When we understand this, we will begin to move forward in Him and pursue our destiny.

He also said in the book of 3 John 1:2, "Beloved, I pray that in all respects you may prosper and be in good health, just as your soul prosper."

Without the knowledge of God's purpose for our lives in Jesus Christ, many will go through life aimlessly. God wants us to be whole and complete, not lacking in anything.

It is through our talents that we will discover our unique purpose in this life.

Purpose is a talent that we are instinctually born with.

The Bible tells us that we are all born with distinct talents or gifts that set us apart.

Chapter Five

HAVE WE FORGOTTEN OUR WAY?

We are the body of Jesus Christ, having many members, but each one has his or her unique ways for serving and bringing glory to the Father. "For we are God's handiwork, created in Jesus Christ to do good works which God prepared in advance for us to do" (Eph. 2:10).

"Every good and perfect gift is from above" (James 1:17).

"Each of you should use whatever gifts you have received to serve others as faithful stewards of God's grace in its various form" (1 Peter 4:10-11).

As I reflect on the story of Moses, I see that God instructed Moses to tell the men to use their gifts for making the temple of the Lord (Ex. 31:3-5).

Some had knowledge of wood from different trees, others knew of materials to make curtains, and others knew how to measure width and length.

Everyone had their gifts to make the temple, and everyone served their purpose for the glory of God.

Exodus 31:3 says, "And I have filled him with the spirit of God, with wisdom, with understanding, with knowledge and with all kinds of skills."

If God called for us to do something, then He will provide the way and everything that we need to get the job done.

We must simply trust in Him and take the limits off of the Almighty, All-knowing, Sovereign God.

We are driven by the demands of life and do not realize that God always has a greater purpose.

His purpose not only encompasses our lives but the lives of those around us at home, work, school, and the surrounding community.

It's important to know and live out our God-given purpose.

We spend nearly every day talking about life and what it means to live.

The Bible tells us that we are created in the image of God and His likeness (Gen. 1:27).

According to Jeremiah 29:11, God has a plan and purpose for our lives.

His purpose is to always help others and bring more clarity to the body of Christ in the surrounding community, for that certain something that defines and integrates our lives.

Purpose is a driving force.

So many people turn to books and other programs for answers to identify their purpose in life.

However, most walk away dissatisfied.

I think everyone feels that pull toward some defining purpose to his or her life, no matter how it may have become overlooked along the way.

In fact, you could say that all forms of life have a phenomenal purpose.

God created mankind with purpose in mind.

Chapter Six

UNDERSTANDING PURPOSE

It is so important that we do not confuse seeking happiness with finding our purpose.

Happiness is what we experience in the daily flow of life.

Waking up with "Purpose"

Purpose is deeper; it is more of an underlying sense of peace and fulfillment overall.

It's a sense of integration and continuous unfolding of our being.

It transcends everyday ups and downs and the disappointments or successes of life. In accordance with our life purpose, we can view all of the above as part of what we encounter along the way.

Purpose does not distract you from that large vision; your ideas, which are like a magnet, steadily pull you toward your destiny and fulfilling your purpose.

Letting go of self-interest opens the door to recognizing our true selves more clearly so we can see whether it is joined

with our outer lives and create a sense of purpose.

Knowing who you are inside—your true values, secrets, desires, imaginations, and capacity for love, empathy, and generosity—relates to and informs your life's purpose.

Purpose calls forth our spirit to serve for something larger than our ego, larger than winning.

The fruits of what we are aiming for take many forms in people.

We are unique, but we are all made in the image of God.

It is in the will of God that we become aware of who we are, what we can do, and what we have in Jesus Christ.

Waking up with "Purpose"

Now, let's briefly look at the beginning of creation and how everything God made served its purpose.

The first book of the Bible, Genesis,

describes how God created the earth.

**In the beginning God created the heavens and earth. Now the earth was formless and empty. Darkness was over the surface of the deep and the spirit of God was hovering over the water. And God said let there be light and there was light. God saw that the light was good. And he separated the light from the darkness. And God called the light day and the darkness he called night.
- Genesis 1:1-5**

As we continue to read, we see that everything that God made was good and served the purpose He had for it.

"God said let us make man in our image, in our likeness and let them rule over the fish of the sea and the birds of the air, over the livestock and all the earth" (Gen. 1:26).

God then made man with purpose attached, giving mankind authority, dominion, and power over the world systems.

Jesus, the Son of God, served His purpose by going to the cross.

John 3:16 tells the story of God's love for mankind.

Waking up with "Purpose"

"For God so loved the world that he gave his only begotten son, that whosoever believe in him should not perish but have ever lasting life."

In 1 Peter chapter 1, it talks about Christ, who truly was foreordained before the foundation of the world but has been revealed in the last times for the sake of you.

His death on Calvary's cross and His resurrection both served as His purpose.

Chapter Seven

LET'S LOOK AT THE CHURCH

This is the point that I want to make clear to every believer.

The body of Jesus Christ has many members, but each member has his or her own way of functioning to serve.

Waking up with "Purpose"

We have to remember that God placed all things under the feet of Jesus, and all power has been given to HHHis name.

Jesus told His disciples, "All authority in heaven and earth has been given to me. Therefore go and make disciples of all nations" (Matt. 28:18-19).

Now if Jesus is the head of His body, which is the church, that same power has been given to the church (Luke 10:19).

By learning the purpose of the church, we can see how to come together as a whole to serve one another and bring a sense of purpose to our lives with understanding.

Now we glorify the Father by living each day in submission to the Lordship of

Jesus Christ and using His spiritual gifts to serve in the five-fold ministry.

Remember that we were created in the very image of God.

So, as we develop a relationship with Him, we will discover our God-given purpose, which will lead us to our destiny.

No one is here aimlessly.

The meaning of the word purpose is to bring us back to our Creator.

Purpose is the reason for which something is done or created, the reason for which something exists.

The reason for mankind's existence is literally to be born as a spirit being into the family of God the Father with purpose while on the earth (Rom. 6:15-16, 8:14-17; Acts 2:39; 2 Peter 3:18; Rev. 3:5-10).

The apostle Paul talked about all he had achieved religiously before being confronted by the risen Christ (Phil. 3:9-10).

Paul's purpose was to know Christ and obtain righteousness through faith in Him, living in fellowship with Him even when it brought on suffering.

Knowing your purpose will strengthen your faith to endure life's issues.

I see that many have walked away from their faith before it could be established.

So many have or are experiencing what we call church hurt.

And for that very reason, the people of God are not aware that they have purpose in this life.

The Father allowed me to see that the same spirit that was on the children of Israel is on today's church.

The sins of the father

For years, the church, which is Jesus's body, has not been functioning in the supernatural life intended for it.

I hear people saying things like, "We do not have to go to church. God sees my heart."

Listen, we are the church!

Making statements like that will unknowingly have us leaving and going back to the old ways of doing things.

The Bible tells us in the book of 2 Corinthians 5:17, "Therefore if anyone is in Christ, he is a new creation. The old things have passed away, behold all things have become new."

We have been reconciled and restored in our relationship with the Father and its assurance that forgiveness of sin is available in Christ.

When we turn and walk away from our faith, we will never discover our God-given purpose, which is what I see happening now.

We have to understand that there is no perfect church.

The body of Christ is made of people like you and me.

We make mistakes because we are humans and not perfect. Sometimes our flesh dictates our actions to us if we are not careful.

That is why it is important to be renewed in our minds in the way we think and lean not to our own understanding.

We must become a group of people who depend on God and are not moved by how things appear to be.

We are the church and the temple for the Holy Spirit to dwell in.

It is so important to read and study God's Word because we all have a part or purpose in the kingdom, and when

Waking up with "Purpose"

we do not fulfill our purpose, the body becomes weaker.

Chapter Eight

FAITH COMES BY HEARING THE WORD OF GOD

The Bible is full of stories of men and women who discovered their purpose. Some did so while facing many storms in their lives.

I believe that is why God told us in the book of Joshua 1:8 to always read and meditate on His Word.

Let's briefly look at a few stories of men and women in the Bible who encountered their purpose.

The story of Moses

Moses was born a Hebrew slave.

When he heard the call to lead the children of Israel from bondage, Moses's purpose was at work.

The great story of Moses has captured the world today, associated with the Ten Commandments.

The story of Esther

Esther, a beautiful Jewish slave girl who caught the king's attention, was able to save her people (Ex. 12:8).

The story of Abraham

When he heard the voice of God saying to leave his land, Abraham stepped out in faith, seeing nothing but dry land. But he trusted that God would lead him, and he became the father of many nations with the blessing of God on his life (Gen. 17:4).

Then there's the story of Joseph.

God had a divine purpose for him. He was hated by his brothers, put into a pit, and sold into slavery, only to be placed second in command to Pharaoh and in the position to save his people from a famine (Gen. 41:41-46).

There are so many more stories in the Bible of people who discovered their purpose, some while facing many trials.

It is important that we make reading our Bible part of our daily bread. When eating God's Word every day, we develop a sense of purpose for our lives.

Having a relationship with the Creator will keep us focused. The enemy tries to use so many distractions to get us off course of what God has purposed for us.

Now faith is the key in pursuing our purpose.

No matter how big or small the assignment is, we have to see ourselves doing what God has called us to do.

It must become our reality.

Distractions can easily mislead us off course. But when we make spending time with God a priority, His Word will lead us back on course and to our destiny.

We need to discover our purpose in life for two reasons.

1. *Fulfilling our purpose gives glory to the Father.*

2. *Knowing our purpose releases us from the captivity of hopelessness and despair.*

Waking up with "Purpose"

Pursuing purpose today, we must recognize that Christ died for all of those who live in Him and they must no longer live for themselves.

God said in Jeremiah 29:11, "For I know the thoughts I have for you declares the Lord. Plans to prosper you and not to harm you. Plans to give you hope and a future."

Joshua 1:8 says, "Do not let this book of the law depart from your mouth.

Meditate on it day and night, so that you may be careful to do everything written in it. Then you will be prosperous and have good success."

Could this be the very reason that so many are lost and have no sense of purpose in life?

I have witnessed countless people who are saved, but they stop right at the door of their salvation.

Once we receive Jesus as Lord and Savior, we do not stop there. He has given the body of believers the keys to the kingdom.

We have to keep moving and seeking God, trusting in Him that there is more.

The story of the children of Israel is a good example of what not to do. Because of their unbelief, they did not trust in God and began to complain. This caused them to miss experiencing the promised land.

Instead, they wandered around aimlessly for forty years.

They made their journey much longer than what God had intended.

Now, does this sound familiar in today's church?

Ask yourselves, what goals or desires within you are you not achieving because of your unbelief or lack of faith?

You must understand that purpose is what drives us to believe and to trust God when He says that He has a plan and a future for us.

He led the children of Israel into the wilderness to develop a new way of thinking for them.

Like the Israelites, we must also learn to trust Him, even when we cannot trace Him.

What is purpose saying?

Stepping out in faith to pursue our assignment takes courage to believe in God and trust that He has called us to do a specific task.

Sometimes the call will be different than what you expected. You might be put into a position where you have never been before.

You might have to go through a wilderness experience, having nothing but your faith that God is with you.

In these times, remember Matthew 6:33. Don't worry, saying, "What are we going to eat or drink," or, "What clothes are we going to wear?" Isn't life more valuable than these things?

Waking up with "Purpose"

Here's another point that I would like to make.

The word "life" in the verse above is talking about how we should not let material things hinder us. A life centered around acquiring material things is a life that will never achieve contentment or lasting happiness.

God will lead us to a place so we can learn that He is only source—to develop the faith that the saints of old had.

No matter where we are in our walk with Him, we must simply trust and believe when he calls.

"And do not be conformed to the pattern of this world, but be ye transformed by the renewing your mind, that you may

prove what is that good and perfect will of God" (Rom. 12:2).

While discovering your purpose, you will realize that it was always a part of you— the very essence of who you are.

As I look at my own children, I see how they are all different and each one has his or her own unique way of doing things.

Their talents or purpose set them apart.

As their mother, I know each one of them and the skills or talents they possess.

Our purpose has to become our reality, recognizing and acknowledging that God has placed those gifts inside of us for the building up of His kingdom.

Waking up with "Purpose"

God has numbered our days, and He will fulfill every purpose He has assigned for us.

When we live a passion-filled life, we are living with purpose.

That feeling that something is missing goes away when we live a passion-filled life.

We can now view everything that God has made and see that He attached purpose to it.

There is nothing on this earth that does not have an assigned purpose.

Sometimes we are so busy that we do not hear what the Spirit of God is saying.

In other words, we need to come to a place where we are willing to submit ourselves to God and acknowledge that He is in control.

When we realize that we are truly incapable of controlling our lives, surrendering becomes easy as pie.

It may be a matter of saying, "Yes, Lord, I trust you."

This will open doors so that we may experience the fullness of all God wants for us.

After all, He is our Creator and has a perfect plan for us when we let Him orchestrate it.

His Word will bring understanding to all that Jesus died so we could know that we have purpose in His kingdom. Shalom.

Pursuing my purpose

I received Jesus as my Savior at six years old, not fully understanding what was going on at that time.

Now, my mother did not take us to church. My siblings and I would ride the big white school bus that picked up all the kids in the surrounding communities.

We were excited because this gave us an opportunity to get out of the house and experience something new. I believe that God was working on me then.

There was no talk about God or Jesus in our home; we would only hear those names when trouble came our way.

The only time that we would hear about Jesus was when my mother's sister

Bonnie Sue would come and visit us from time to time.

On one of her visits, she was reading her Bible, and it caught my attention, so I began to ask her questions.

All of a sudden, I heard her laugh and laugh. Then she said, "Lord, my niece is seeking You!" and right then and there, she began to pray for me.

I believe that in that moment when my auntie prayed over me, my life changed and was never the same. God has always used a ram in the brush. Amen.

When I heard the call

I want to share just a brief part of my testimony and my journey.

Waking up with "Purpose"

As mentioned earlier, the Spirit of God found me at the lowest part of my life. I was on drugs and confused and lost, but at times, I would cry out to Him because I was in a place that I didn't want to be. I had seven children who needed me, and I wanted a better life for us. So, He met me where I was. Yes, He came down into the pit of hell and saved me. He cleaned me up and turned my life around. I then began to pursue my desire of becoming a nurse. God's favor was on my life, and He allowed me to go back to school to receive my medical license. Life was good. Yes, for the first time in my life, I was living for me and my kids. I was going higher in my career and wanted to pursue working for the city of Los Angeles as a paramedic. Yes, I was on my way, so I thought...until I learned that I was not in His will, His perfect will. And

then came the storms of life and losing everything.

In my early twenties, I began to search for the unknown God.

When I attended church service, I would hear people talk about the God who I wanted to know about.

They would preach, speak in tongues, and lay hands on people.

But still, there was no understanding.

I knew that people would go to church to feel better, but I was empty on the inside...clueless.

My life became like a seesaw, going up and down, but deep inside of me. I knew that I had to go to church to learn about who God was and to fellowship with other believers.

Around 1978, I was fellowship with mature women in my community as they went out witnessing about God. This was my first experience doing something like this.

I was not aware at that time that my own purpose was at work.

I was going out with these women because it was the right thing to do.

But in 2000, while in my oldest daughter's room, I remember hearing a still, small voice as I looked out the window, asking, "What are you looking at?"

Right then and there, I knew that I was about to have a God moment.

A moment of silence and peace came over me. I answered and said, "I see kids playing and people walking up and down the streets, cars passing by—I see life."

Then that same still, small voice said, "Yes, life! But they are living without a clue as to who I am...who will go?"

I wasn't sure of what was happening in that moment, But as I stood there at a standstill, the Spirit of God began to witness to my spirit.

Then I said, "I will go, Lord."

I didn't know exactly what was going to happen, but I knew that God was calling me to go.

Years had passed since my encounter with the Lord, and all of a sudden, that same still, small voice said, "Go out and be a witness for Me."

Fear came in, and I begin to ignore what I had heard until it kept pulling on my spirit, compelling me to go.

So, I began to go and pass out flyers with the scripture John 3:16 on them in the surrounding communities.

You see, I had to step out of my own comfort zone and trust that I had heard the call.

From that moment, a ministry of spreading the Word and taking it to the streets was birthed out of me.

And those who lived around me, including gang members, drug dealers, prostitutes, and homeless people were the ones who I was led to share the good news of Jesus Christ with.

So, witnessing for the love of God and others became a part of my life. Some of the gang members received Christ as their Lord and Savior, and their lives have been transformed. Oh, glory to God! (see purpose at work!)

The Spirit of God will have you grow from one level to another and from faith to faith in Him.

He will allow us to be tested beyond our natural abilities.

I would walk through my community sharing the Word of God, and people

began to recognize me and what I was doing.

My neighbors would ask me to come to their house and pray for whatever was going on in their lives at the time.

I had Bible studies in my home, even though I really did not fully understand the Bible.

I would go to malls and pass out flyers with John 3:16 on them as well. I just wanted to be a vessel for the Lord.

Then the unthinkable happened.

... The storms of life

The believers of Jesus Christ will face some storms or trials in this walk.

"In this world ye shall have tribulations... but be of good cheer, I have overcome the world" (John 16:33).

Then I started losing everything that I had worked so hard for. Keep in mind that I was serving in my church and tithing and fellowshipping with other believers.

As I mention earlier, I was doing okay on my journey, working in the field I desired.

But yet, I was stripped of everything, and I mean everything.

Losing everything caused me and my kids to become homeless.

Staying in some of the most unthinkable hotels, we had to endure some painful situations, and as a mother, this was not easy.

Not fully understanding why this was happening to me, I began to seek and inquire of the Lord on a whole new level.

Life just got real for me.

I wasn't until then that I got to a place in my mind where I wanted to know God for myself.

I was invited to attend a church service at Crenshaw Christian Center, known as "The Faith Dome," and the guest speaker was Dr. Juanita Bynum. Now this woman spoke the Word of God like I had never heard before. She got my attention!

She began to say that people expect God to heal them or bless them financially, but they are not operating in the faith of the Word of God.

They have no real fellowship with Him according to His Word.

Then she said that God is only going to move according to His Word—not our tears or any other emotions that we might have.

He told us that His Word will not return to Him void (Isa. 55:11).

I began to seek God more for understanding. My thirst was increasing.

My life was now headed in a new direction, and I was drawn closer to fellowship with Him on a new level as I began to get into His Word.

I hadn't been walking in faith, but I knew that I had to trust in Him if I was going to abide in Him.

I heard about faith but did not really understand how it worked.

Like so many people, I complained and cried out to God for answers concerning my life and what was going on.

We have to understand that once we receive Jesus as Lord over our lives, we will be headed in a new direction, a path that will be tested by fire (1 Peter 1:7).

Without faith, it is impossible to please God, and those who come to Him must first believe that He rewards those who seek Him (Heb. 11:6).

We can easily praise God when everything is going good, but that is not true faith.

Sometimes we might have to endure some longsuffering for the process to be completed.

I became aware that my purpose was going out and taking the Word of God to the streets.

Knowing this gave me confidence and strength that I needed; it was part of who I was.

I began to tap into my purpose!

We all have a God-given purpose in this life, but without understanding His Word, we will go through life aimlessly, and I had had enough.

So, I began to get intimate with the Lord, shutting everything down around me so I would hear Him clearly.

Then the Holy Spirit led me on a twenty-one-day fast. During those days, I wasn't doing what I would normally do—no food, no water, no TV, and I didn't talk too much. I had to deny my flesh and bring it under subjection to the Word of God.

In that time of seeking Him, God begin to show me the church and its state on the earth, compromising with unclean spirits.

By this action, the church has turned away from God.

This has caused a shift to take place in the believer's walk.

As I continued to read the story of the children of Israel and how they kept doubting God by letting the pressures of life consume them, I saw similarities in how we worry about what we are going to eat or drink and how we are going to pay bills and rent. This mindset caused a spirit of depression to come upon them, and the same spirit has come upon today's church.

Then I began to feel the spirit of heaviness on my heart like never before, and a great cry for Zion came upon me to weep for God's people, including myself.

Then I began to hear the word "purpose."

It kept ringing louder and louder in my spirit.

I asked myself what the Lord was saying to me, and as I got closer to Him, He began to reveal to me what was going on with believers.

I continued to witness to others, sharing my testimony and discussing who we are and what Jesus did for us by dying on the cross.

But the church is not functioning or operating at its fullness.

Matthew 5:13 tells us that we are the salt of the world, but if the salt loses its flavor, what good is it?

We have the authority, dominion, and power to take back everything that the enemy has stolen.

Yes, Jesus has already paid the price. Just because the Lord doesn't move when we expect Him to doesn't mean He is not able. We must trust and believe that God and His Word are one, and He is not a man that He should lie.

"The kingdom of God suffereth violence, and the violence take it back by force" (Matt. 11:12).

Now in the darkest time of my life, I had heard the word "purpose."

But I could not believe that God had called a person like me—a person who hadn't finished college.

But I had to move in faith while facing some of my most difficult trials ever. I knew that the Lord was calling me to step out of my comfort zone and fellowship

with the Holy Spirit, so I had to keep my eyes looking to the hills where my help comes from.

I had to learn quickly that the enemy will use whomever and whatever he can to distract me to get me off course.

I had to listen and trust God that in He was in complete control in every situation.

I sensed that if I turned to look at what was going on in my life, somehow the enemy would try and sneak in and bring things to my mind. But the Holy Spirit had begun a new work in me...oh, bless His holy name.

My faith was increasing, and I was not going to let the devil win...no, not this time.

So, the fire got hotter in pursuing my purpose.

I then realized that I was right where God needed me to be so I could seek Him and develop the kind of faith that Hebrews 11 talks about.

The Holy Spirit began to show me who I was and that writing has always has been a part of me.

Throughout my life, I loved writing. I would write down things that came to my mind or when I heard something that sounded good.

I would write poems and songs, and at one time in my life, I had started to write a book, but I realized that it wasn't the right time.

Waking up with "Purpose"

I learned that everything has a season— that's how God operates.

Now, was it easy? No.

I had to submit to God with a complete yes.

Knowing that I love to write, I just could not believe that the almighty God was going to use me because He knew my past. But He also knows my future.

He reminded me about the children of Israel and how they had wandered around aimlessly, telling me to be careful and not lean on my own understanding, but rather acknowledge Him so He could guide my steps.

I said out loud, "Lord, do You see where I am? It's dark outside, and there's so much pain."

With so many distractions around me, I had to find that secret place and take refuge in Him so I could hear. His Word remined me that He has a plan and a future for my life and that my suffering had purpose.

What the enemy intends for evil, the Lord will turn around for our good (Gen. 50:20).

Yes, we may endure some suffering while pursuing our purpose for the kingdom; Jesus also suffered on His way to the cross.

I had to speak God's Word over my life in order for me to fulfill my destiny.

We are to always walk by faith and not by sight.

"And when the enemy comes in like a flood, the spirit of God shall lift up a standard against him" (Isa. 59:19).

I had to realize that if God allowed the pain and suffering, then it must serve for His purpose.

I also learned that before we can move into ministry, we have to learn to love and forgive those who have caused us pain.

The Lord began to work on me. He allowed me to be tested in an area that I had never been in before. I was placed in a dark place, and in order for me to see the light, I had to trust God. And let me tell you, this was by far the most traumatic experience ever.

Yet in that traumatized state of mind, I had to remain in the Word of God and not let my emotions take charge based on how I was feeling.

The Lord spoke to me and said, "Pray for that person."

He was letting me know right then and there that I was to pray for those who had deceived me and spoken all matters of evil against me. This was part of my assignment while I was on my journey.

I had to act and move quickly in the spirit of love from my heart because only God can see the heart of man...glory.

The Lord reminded me that He was preparing me and that He had allowed certain things in my life to mature me in my walk with Him and help me understand that there will always be suffering before ministry.

Waking up with "Purpose"

It is so important that we know where we are in Him so that when trials come or the issues of life become unbearable, we will be found rooted in His Word of faith.

Without doing so, we will never discover our purpose because we will be walking in the wrong direction.

Purpose

Loneliness is not the absent of people, but of purpose.

If you are reading this book, then my purpose has been fulfilled. Glory to God!

Written on the back

In the year of 2014, I heard in my spirit, "Do not worry about what you are going to eat, drink, or wear." Not sure of what

to think about what I'd heard, I began to ignore it, but I still kept on hearing it.

Then I knew that the Lord was speaking to me.

I responded by saying, "Lord, what do You mean? I am a woman—I have to keep myself up!" That was the first thing that came to my mind. Like so many others, I was only thinking of material things.

At this time, I had lost my job and then my car and apartment, forcing me to move in with my daughter.

I started to go out and look for work because I was a grown woman and was not about to stay living with my daughter.

Job interview after job interview, but still nothing!

At this time, my health was getting also getting attacked, and no job meant no insurance. Everything tried to hinder or stop me.

I heard again, "Do not worry about what you are going to eat or drink or wear. You are going to learn that I am the only source that you need."

It hit me that I would not have to worry because I would have the money to take care of my needs and wants.

I knew then that I had to surrender myself as a vessel to be used by the Lord.

Yes, the Lord meant business, and I had to move quickly in faith and trust in Him.

As I look at it now, how else could I tell anyone to trust in the Lord when times get hard or when the issues of life happen?

We cannot minister to anyone without experience being our first teacher. So, I had to "wake up with a purpose."

I pray that the Holy Spirit will lead you on your new journey as you began to seek for your purpose in the kingdom of God.

I encourage you to write them down.

Remember that your purpose is the very essence of who you are.

I also encourage you to establish a relationship with the One who created you and to get involved in your church. Even if you do not know your purpose at this time, God will reveal it to you.

Waking up with "Purpose"

Remember that faith without works is dead (James 2:14-26).

Habakkuk 2:2 tells us to write down our vision and make it plain so we may run with it.

Prayer

Our father who art in heaven, hallowed be thy name. Thy kingdom come, thy will be done, on earth as it is in heaven. Give us this day our daily bread and forgive us our trespasses, as we forgive those who trespass against us.

Lead us not into temptation but deliver us from evil...for thine is the kingdom and the power and the glory forever and ever. Amen.

In the name of Jesus, I pray for every believer who is drawn to fellowship with You, Father, by reading this book.

Father, anoint every word that will alter their lives.

Let Your Spirit lead them to a fellowship with You like never before.

Father, I pray for the supernatural to occur in their walk with You and that they will begin to step out in faith and have confidence in pursuing their purpose.

Father, reveal to them that they are members of Your kingdom and that when we are not aware of our purpose, the kingdom cannot function as a whole.

Knowing your purpose will unlock doors that have been shut.

Waking up with "Purpose"

What...is...your...purpose!

In the back of this book are a few blank pages for you to begin to write down your thoughts and ideas while you are on your journey.

Be encouraged in pursuing your purpose.

Written by: jamye l. Hill

www.ingramcontent.com/pod-product-compliance
Ingram Content Group UK Ltd.
Pitfield, Milton Keynes, MK11 3LW, UK
UKHW041944230426
12048UKWH00008B/133